RIFF BY RIFF:
THE BEATLES

ISBN 0-634-01127-8

7777 W. BLUEMOUND RD. P.O. BOX 13819 MILWAUKEE, WI 53213

Visit Hal Leonard Online at
www.halleonard.com

Music arranged by Martin Shellard
Additional text and editing by Derek Jones
All recording and guitars by Martin Shellard
Music processed by Paul Ewers Music Design
Cover design by Johnson Banks
Photographs courtesy of London Features International

CONTENTS

"There was a magic chemistry that happened between us and somehow it got into the grooves on those records. Not every song we ever did was brilliant, but a lot of them are timeless, great songs that happen to have a chemistry in the grooves which appeals to each generation as it comes up."
George Harrison

RIFF BY RIFF...THE BEATLES

Learning Is Easy When You Know How!

How often do you see a guitarist in a band - amateur or professional - using sheet music?

Very rarely, if ever at all! So how do they remember all those songs, with so many different notes, phrases and solos?

Simple - by breaking each song down into manageable, easy to learn chunks, typically eight bars or so long. You are probably already familiar with the names given to these sections - verse, chorus, bridge, middle eight, and so on.

Each of these sections is made up of smaller passages or 'building blocks' - these are known as riffs.

That's what this book is all about - learning to play a song bit by bit using these building blocks or riffs, then putting them together in the correct order.

It's All In The Riffs!

You will immediately begin learning songs by playing the individual riffs that make up each song. These fall into two types - 'riffs' and 'rhythm riffs'.

Riffs are short, melodic phrases, usually repeated a number of times throughout a song. Riffs are often a song's most instantly recognisable trademark - the seven note riff that kicks off 'Layla', for example - so mastering them is essential.

Rhythm riffs are chord-based patterns that underpin the structure of a song and can be just as crucial. A good example would be the underlining rhythm riffs that propel each verse of the classic 'Sultans Of Swing'.

Each riff is notated in both standard and tab notation, while the rhythm riffs appear as guitar chord boxes with the relevant rhythms below.

The riffs are presented in the order in which they appear in the song and each one comes with an explanation, offering help on how to play it. Listen to the relevant track number on the CD for a demonstration of how each riff should sound.

The Route To Success

Once you have got to grips with all the riffs of a song, it's time to link them all together using the second section - the 'Riff Route Map'.

This clearly displays the structure of each song, showing you exactly where to play each of the riffs you have learned. These maps are also collected together in a special pull-out section for ease of use. There are handy markers to help keep you on track, such as lyric cues and timing boxes, which relate directly to the music on the CD.

Now here's the good part - as well as featuring audio examples of how every riff should sound in isolation, the CD also contains full-length song demonstrations and complete backing tracks for you to practice your riffs to, play each guitar part or simply to jam along with! When used in conjunction with these audio tracks, the Riff Route Map makes it clear exactly how all the different elements of the song are brought together.

Following each Riff Route Map is a complete lyric guide with guitar boxes and chord symbols, presenting a quick and useful one-page reference to all the lyrics and chord changes for each song.

Are You Ready To Play?

Each book in the 'Riff By Riff' series not only teaches you the essential riffs from the greatest songs by some of the world's finest guitarists and bands, it also gives you an inside look at the techniques, skills and secrets of each player.

With authentic tablature transcriptions, CD demonstrations and backing tracks, notes on how to play each riff, in-depth technique advice and guidance on how to get the right sound, 'Riff By Riff' gives you a complete and thorough breakdown of how to play in the style of your favourite guitarist.

Now that's the introduction dispensed with, get ready to riff!

Guitar Tablature Explained

Guitar music can be notated three different ways: on a musical stave, in tablature, and in rhythm slashes

RHYTHM SLASHES are written above the stave. Strum chords in the rhythm indicated. Round noteheads indicate single notes.

THE MUSICAL STAVE shows pitches and rhythms and is divided by lines into bars. Pitches are named after the first seven letters of the alphabet.

TABLATURE graphically represents the guitar fingerboard. Each horizontal line represents a string, and each number represents a fret.

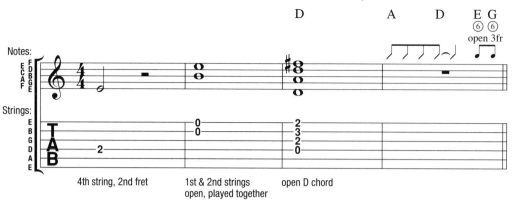

4th string, 2nd fret   1st & 2nd strings open, played together   open D chord

definitions for special guitar notation

SEMI-TONE BEND: Strike the note and bend up a semi-tone (1/2 step).

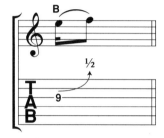

WHOLE-TONE BEND: Strike the note and bend up a whole-tone (whole step).

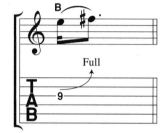

GRACE NOTE BEND: Strike the note and bend as indicated. Play the first note as quickly as possible.

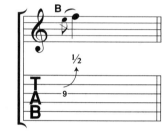

QUARTER-TONE BEND: Strike the note and bend up a 1/4 step.

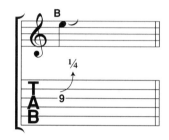

BEND & RELEASE: Strike the note and bend up as indicated, then release back to the original note.

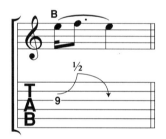

COMPOUND BEND & RELEASE: Strike the note and bend up and down in the rhythm indicated.

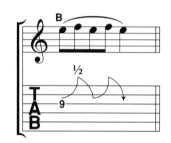

PRE-BEND: Bend the note as indicated, then strike it.

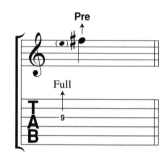

PRE-BEND & RELEASE: Bend the note as indicated. Strike it and release the note back to the original pitch.

UNISON BEND: Strike the two notes simultaneously and bend the lower note up to the pitch of the higher.

BEND & RESTRIKE: Strike the note and bend as indicated then restrike the string where the symbol occurs.

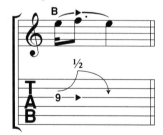

BEND, HOLD AND RELEASE: Same as bend and release but hold the bend for the duration of the tie.

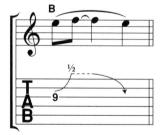

BEND AND TAP: Bend the note as indicated and tap the higher fret while still holding the bend.

VIBRATO: The string is vibrated by rapidly bending and releasing the note with the fretting hand.

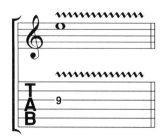

HAMMER-ON: Strike the first (lower) note with one finger, then sound the higher note (on the same string) with another finger by fretting it without picking.

PULL-OFF: Place both fingers on the notes to be sounded, Strike the first note and without picking, pull the finger off to sound the second (lower) note.

LEGATO SLIDE (GLISS): Strike the first note and then slide the same fret-hand finger up or down to the second note. The second note is not struck.

NOTE: The speed of any bend is indicated by the music notation and tempo.

SHIFT SLIDE (GLISS & RESTRIKE): Same as legato slide, except the second note is struck.

TRILL: Very rapidly alternate between the notes indicated by continuously hammering on and pulling off.

TAPPING: Hammer ("tap") the fret indicated with the pick-hand index or middle finger and pull off to the note fretted by the fret hand.

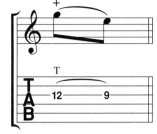

PICK SCRAPE: The edge of the pick is rubbed down (or up) the string, producing a scratchy sound.

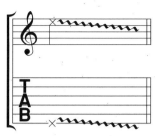

MUFFLED STRINGS: A percussive sound is produced by laying the fret hand across the string(s) without depressing, and striking them with the pick hand.

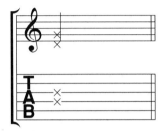

NATURAL HARMONIC: Strike the note while the fret-hand lightly touches the string directly over the fret indicated.

PINCH HARMONIC: The note is fretted normally and a harmonic is produced by adding the edge of the thumb or the tip of the index finger of the pick hand to the normal pick attack.

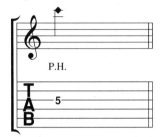

HARP HARMONIC: The note is fretted normally and a harmonic is produced by gently resting the pick hand's index finger directly above the indicated fret (in parentheses) while the pick hand's thumb or pick assists by plucking the appropriate string.

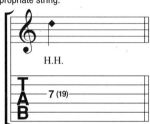

PALM MUTING: The note is partially muted by the pick hand lightly touching the string(s) just before the bridge.

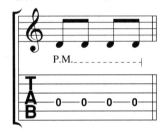

RAKE: Drag the pick across the strings indicated with a single motion.

TREMOLO PICKING: The note is picked as rapidly and continuously as possible.

ARPEGGIATE: Play the notes of the chord indicated by quickly rolling them from bottom to top.

SWEEP PICKING: Rhythmic downstroke and/or upstroke motion across the strings.

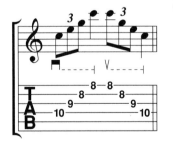

VIBRATO DIVE BAR AND RETURN: The pitch of the note or chord is dropped a specific number of steps (in rhythm) then returned to the original pitch.

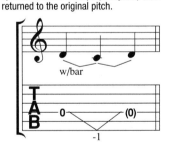

VIBRATO BAR SCOOP: Depress the bar just before striking the note, then quickly release the bar.

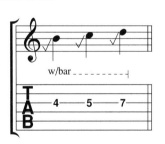

VIBRATO BAR DIP: Strike the note and then immediately drop a specific number of steps, then release back to the original pitch.

additional musical definitions

> (accent)	• Accentuate note (play it louder).	
∧ (accent)	• Accentuate note with great intensity.	
(staccato)	• Shorten time value of note.	
⊓	• Downstroke	
V	• Upstroke	

D.%. al Coda

D.C. al Fine

tacet

1. **2.**

- Go back to the sign (%), then play until the bar marked *To Coda* ⊕ then skip to the section marked ⊕ *Coda*.

- Go back to the beginning of the song and play until the bar marked *Fine* (end).

- Instrument is silent (drops out).

- Repeat bars between signs.

- When a repeated section has different endings, play the first ending only the first time and the second ending only the second time.

NOTE: Tablature numbers in parentheses mean:
1. The note is sustained, but a new articulation (such as hammer on or slide) begins.
2. A note may be fretted but not necessarily played.

I FEEL FINE

'I Feel Fine' topped both the UK and US charts in 1964; a year which saw The Beatles consolidate their position at the top of the world of pop.

A song which glances back to earlier styles, it owes much of its vigour to the rather basic recording facilities of the day. The style of guitar playing on this track, although a little rough around the edges, is full of life and spontaneity. Once you've got the riffs under your fingers, try to keep the energy flowing from beginning to end, perhaps taking your cue from the effervescent rhythm section!

Riff 1

All the riffs in this song are based around the barre E chord shape. To make the riffs easier, hold down the chord before you begin playing and then let the notes ring. Although there are a lot of two note chords, you should try to make the top notes stand out as these form the melody line. To help you achieve this, follow the picking directions; the upstrokes will make you play the top notes louder.

Watch out for the stretch with your fourth finger in the second bar of each phrase (e.g. the E in bar 2) – you don't need to keep the whole chord down when you play this note but you should hold the A note that's played with it.

There are two guitar sounds associated with this riff; the first is George Harrison's hollowbody Gretsch which has a big, warm sound – then towards the end of the riff John joins in with a brighter Rickenbacker sound. Use a clean tone with the neck pickup for the first half, then a middle or bridge position for the rest.

Riff 2

TRACK 2

Riff 2 is similar to Riff 1 but uses only the G and D chord shapes. As in Riff 1, when the progression moves down to the G chord you'll have to change the fingering for the second bar of the phrase. Instead of using a fourth finger stretch it's much easier to change position and use an open string.

Riff 3

TRACK 3

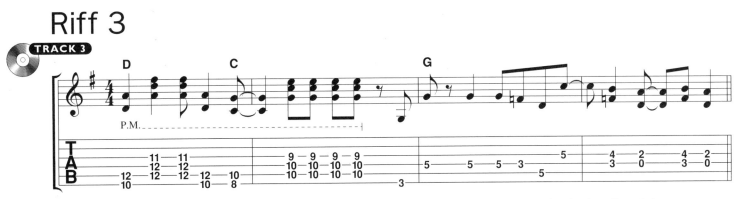

The first two bars of the chorus have a more laid back feel to them. Dampen the strings lightly with your palm and feel free to vary the rhythm. Bars 3-4 have a similar pattern to Riff 1.

Rhythm Riff 1

TRACK 4

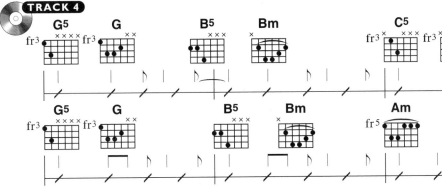

This rhythm riff is used for the bridge section. As you play G5 followed by G hold down the whole chord, striking only the bottom two strings for the first chord – this gives some variety to the riff. Play the chords lightly and unobtrusively.

Riff 4

TRACK 5

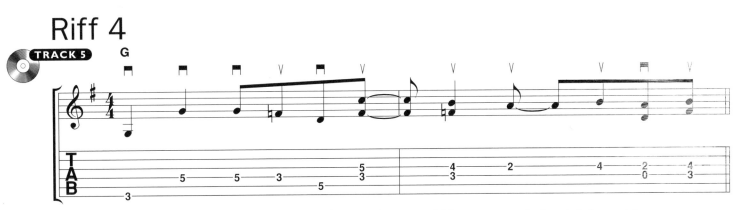

This riff is used for the outro section and is basically the same as the patterns used in Riffs 1 and 2. Use the same picking pattern as before to bring out the top notes.

I FEEL FINE
Riff Route Map

TRACK 6 Full version   TRACK 7 Backing track only

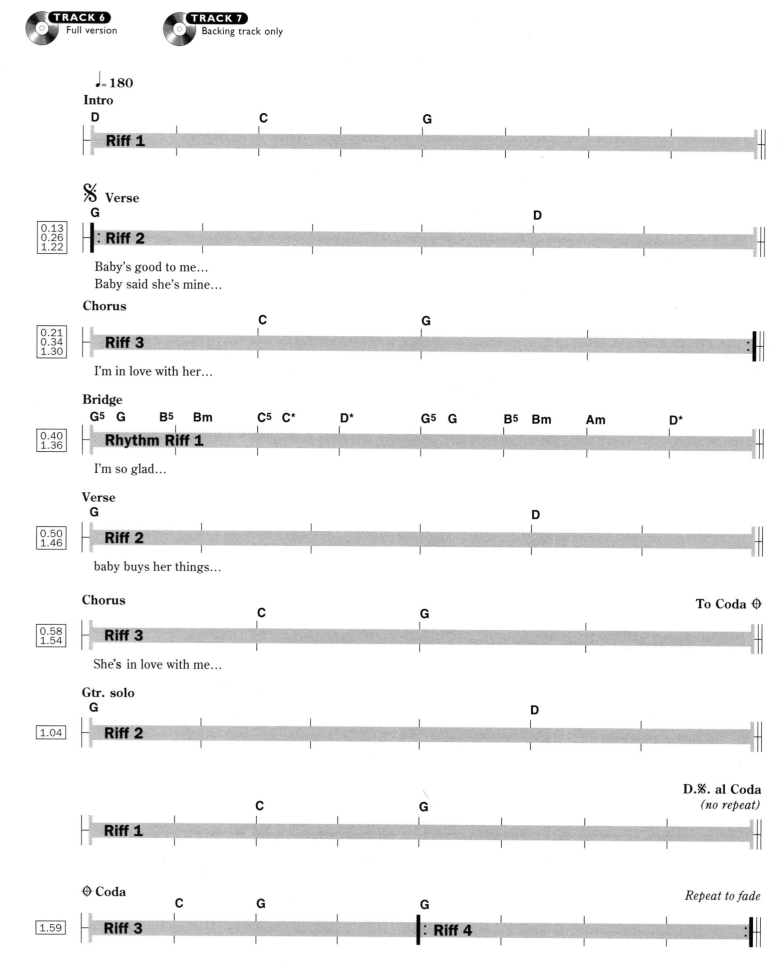

I FEEL FINE
Lyrics

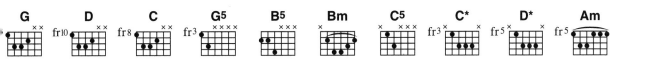

G   **D**   **C**   **G5**   **B5**   **Bm**   **C5**   **C***   **D***   **Am**

Intro: 8 bars

G
Verse 1:   Baby's good to me, you know
She's happy as can be, you know
D
She said so.

C   **G**
Chorus: I'm in love with her and I feel fine.

Verse 2:   Baby says she's mine, you know
She tells me all the time, you know
D
She said so.

C   **G**
Chorus: I'm in love with her and I feel fine.

G5 G B5 Bm   C5 C*   **D***
Bridge: I'm so glad that she's my little girl
G5 G   B5 Bm   Am
She's so glad she's telling all the
D*
world.

G
Verse 3:   That her baby buys her things, you
know
He buys her diamond rings, you
know
D
She said so.

C   **G**
Chorus: She's in love with me and I feel fine.

Instr: 14 bars

G
Verse 4:   Baby says she's mine, you know
She tells me all the time, you know
D
She said so.

C   **G**
Chorus: I'm in love with her and I feel fine.

G5 G B5 Bm   C5 C*   **D***
Bridge: I'm so glad that she's my little girl
G5 G   B5 Bm   Am
She's so glad she's telling all the
D*
world.

G
Verse 5:   That her baby buys her things, you
know
He buys her diamond rings, you
know
D
She said so.

C   **G**
Chorus: She's in love with me and I feel fine,
C   **G**
She's in love with me and I feel fine.

TICKET TO RIDE

Words and Music by John Lennon & Paul McCartney

Recorded in 1965, 'Ticket To Ride' broke new ground for The Beatles with its huge electric guitar sound, and pointed firmly towards the more psychedelic compositions of the future.

The main riff in this song needs to be stated boldly at first, and then brought back slightly to accommodate the vocals. Again, feel is all important once you've learnt all the riffs – this track has plenty of scope for ad libs to allow you to bring your own interpretation to the music.

Riff 1a

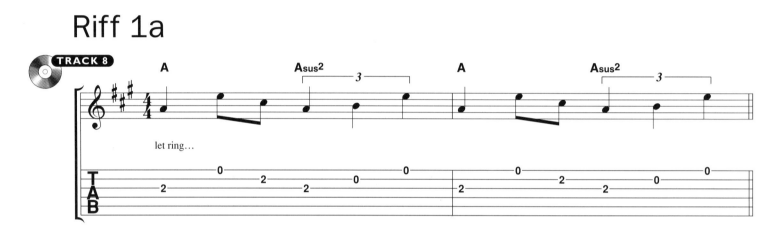

This is another chord based riff, this time using the open A and Asus2 chord shapes. Use your first and second fingers to hold down the G and B strings so you can keep the notes ringing.

The guitar used on the recording is an electric 12-string which gives the riff a bright, jangly sound; but it will also sound good on a 6-string if you play with a clean tone and use the bridge pickup.

Riff 2

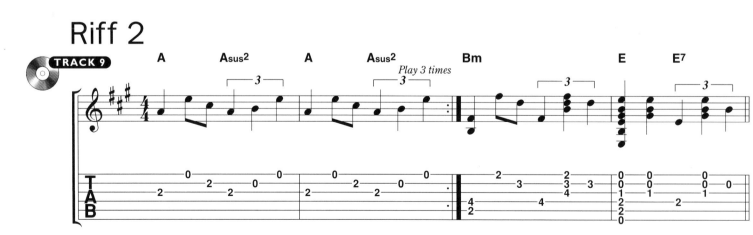

This riff starts off like Riff 1a, but has two bars of heavier chords tacked on at the end. Don't worry about playing these two bars exactly as written – The

Beatles' songs often have some ad lib rhythm parts after a strong riff – it allows the vocal melody to stand out.

Rhythm Riff 1

TRACK 10

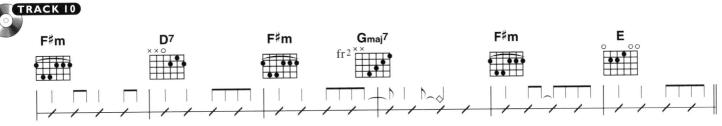

This is another riff that can be played ad lib. Once again, the guitar hangs back to leave room for the vocal. On the recording the Gmaj7 chord is played by a 6-string guitar (in the centre of the mix).

Rhythm Riff 2

TRACK 11

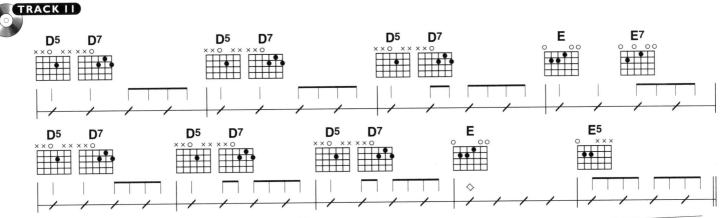

For greater contrast in the bridge section, play this riff with more attack and a stricter rhythm and make the final bar build into the verse.

Riff 1b

TRACK 12

This riff resembles Riff 1a but stops abruptly with an A chord on the first beat of bar 2.

Rhythm Riff 3

TRACK 13

Repeat to fade

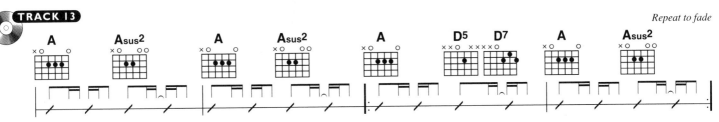

The feel of this riff is based on the rhythm of Riff 1a. You can vary the rhythm of the outro as much as you like, using this riff as a guide.

TICKET TO RIDE
Riff Route Map

TRACK 14
Full version

TRACK 15
Backing track only

♩ = 124

Intro

| A | Asus² | A | Asus² | A | Asus² | A | Asus² |

Riff 1a

I

Verse

| A | Asus² | A | Asus² | A | Asus² | A | Asus² | A | Asus² | A | Asus² | Bm | E | E⁷ |

0.18 — Riff 2

think I'm gonna be sad…

Chorus

| F♯m | D⁷ | F♯m | Gmaj⁷ | F♯m | E | A | Asus² | A | Asus² |

0.27 — Rhythm Riff 1 ... Riff 1a

She's got a ticket to ride…

She

𝄋 Verse

| A | Asus² | A | Asus² | A | Asus² | A | Asus² | A | Asus² | A | Asus² | Bm | E | E⁷ |

0.42 / 1.31 / 2.19 — Riff 2

1.3. said that…
2. think I'm gonna be sad…

Chorus

| F♯m | D⁷ | F♯m | Gmaj⁷ | F♯m | E | A | Asus² | A | Asus² |

To Coda ⊕

0.58 / 1.46 / 2.34 — Rhythm Riff 1 ... Riff 1a

She's got a ticket to ride…

I

Bridge

| D⁵ D⁷ | D⁵ D⁷ | D⁵ D⁷ | E | E⁷ | D⁵ D⁷ | D⁵ D⁷ | D⁵ D⁷ | E | E⁵ |

2° D.𝄋. al Coda

1.13 / 2.02 — Rhythm Riff 2

don't know why she's…

She

⊕ Coda

| A | Asus² | A | A | Asus² | A | Asus² | A | D⁷ | A | Asus² |

2.50

Repeat to fade

Riff 1b ... Rhythm Riff 3

My baby don't care…

TICKET TO RIDE
Lyrics

A   Asus2   Bm   E   E7   F#m   D7   fr2 Gmaj7   D5   E5

Intro: 4 bars

Verse 1:
     A   Asus2   A
I think I'm going to be sad
     Asus2   A Asus2 A   Asus2
I think it's today,   yeah.
       A   Asus2   A
The girl that's driving me mad
     Asus2   Bm   E   E7
Is going away.

Chorus:
    F#m   D7
She's got a ticket to ride,
    F#m   Gmaj7
She's got a ticket to ri-i-ide,
    F#m   E
She's got a ticket to ride,
          A Asus2 A Asus2
And she don't care.

Verse 2:
      A   Asus2   A
She said that living with me
     Asus2   A Asus2 A Asus2
Was bringing her down,   yeah.
    A   Asus2   A
She would never be free
     Asus2   Bm   E   E7
When I was around.

Chorus:
    F#m   D7
She's got a ticket to ride,
    F#m   Gmaj7
She's got a ticket to ri-i-ide,
    F#m   E
She's got a ticket to ride,
          A Asus2 A Asus2
And she don't care.

Bridge:
    D5 D7 etc.
I don't know why she's riding so high
She ought to think twice
                E   E7
She ought to do right by me.
    D5 D7 etc.
Before she gets to sayin' goodbye
She ought to think twice
                E   E5
She ought to do right by me.

Verse 3:
     A   Asus2   A
I think I'm going to be sad
     Asus2   A Asus2 A   Asus2
I think it's today,   yeah.
       A   Asus2   A
The girl that's driving me mad
     Asus2   Bm   E
Is going away.

Chorus:
    F#m   D7
She's got a ticket to ride,
    F#m   Gmaj7
She's got a ticket to ri-i-ide,
    F#m   E
She's got a ticket to ride,
          A Asus2 A Asus2
And she don't care.

Bridge:
    D5 D7 etc.
I don't know why she's riding so high
She ought to think twice
                E   E7
She ought to do right by me
    D5 D7 etc.
Before she gets to sayin' goodbye
She ought to think twice
                E   E5
She ought to do right by me.

Verse 4:
      A   Asus2   A
She said that living with me
     Asus2   A Asus2 A Asus2
Was bringing her down,   yeah.
    A   Asus2   A
She would never be free
     Asus2   Bm   E   E7
When I was around.

Chorus:
    F#m   D7
She's got a ticket to ride,
    F#m   Gmaj7
She's got a ticket to ri-i-ide,
    F#m   E
She's got a ticket to ride,
          A Asus2 A
And she don't care.

Fade:
               A Asus2
My baby don't care.

DAY TRIPPER

Words and Music by John Lennon & Paul McCartney

This blues-based psychedelic single, issued at the
end of 1965, marks the start of more explicit drug
references in The Beatles' lyrics.

The song starts with an instantly memorable guitar
riff which is repeated throughout the song in several
different keys. The bass reinforces this riff
throughout each verse and is a useful guide when
learning the guitar part. In this deceptively simple
song, the guitar lines must be played with fluidity to
match the smooth vocal lines. A great part for any
guitarist to have in their repertoire.

Riff 1

The best way to play this riff is to keep your first
finger at the second fret. This means that the first
two fretted notes are played by the third and fourth
fingers while the next two are played with a third
finger barre on the A and D strings. If you keep to
this one finger per fret approach and use alternate
picking it should be easy to keep this riff rolling.

The sound is typical of early Harrison – clean and fat
but still twangy. Use the middle or neck pickup
position with a warm clean tone.

Riff 2

Riff 1 is extended into Riff 2 for the verse section.
Use the same pattern for the E chord, then simply
move it up a string for the A7, using the same
fingering.

"I was rhythm guitarist. It's an important
job. I can make a band drive."
John Lennon

Riff 3

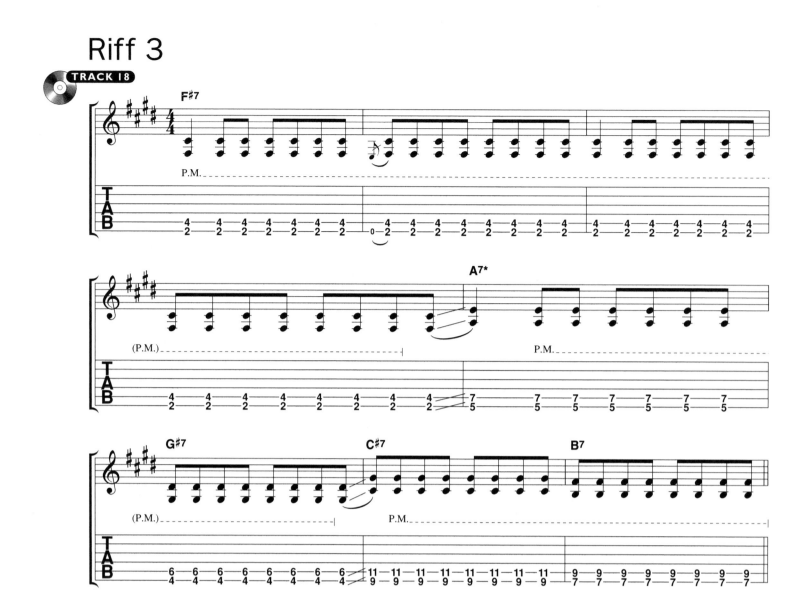

This chugging power-chord riff underpins the chorus. Use the slides and hammer-ons to break up the repeated chords.

Riff 4

Although this is similar to Riffs 1 and 2, you'll need to change the fingering because there are no open strings. Use your fourth finger to slide up to D♯ then barre the D and G strings with your first finger. Finally, still using the first finger, play the A. The sound for this bridge section is slightly distorted, so use the bridge pickup with an overdriven tone.

Riff 5

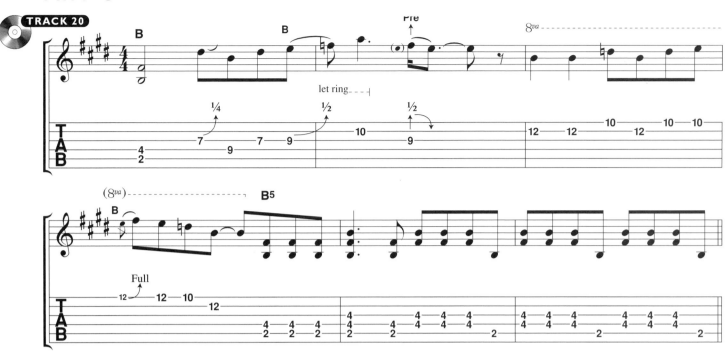

Riff 5 starts as a melodic guitar solo. Make sure that you hold the bent G string in bar 2, as you play the A on the top string. This should be played with a clean tone.

"The anchor that always held us was our musicality. We were pretty good musicians, in a smallish way, perhaps, but we were a good little rhythm section and a good little band."
Paul McCartney

DAY TRIPPER
Riff Route Map

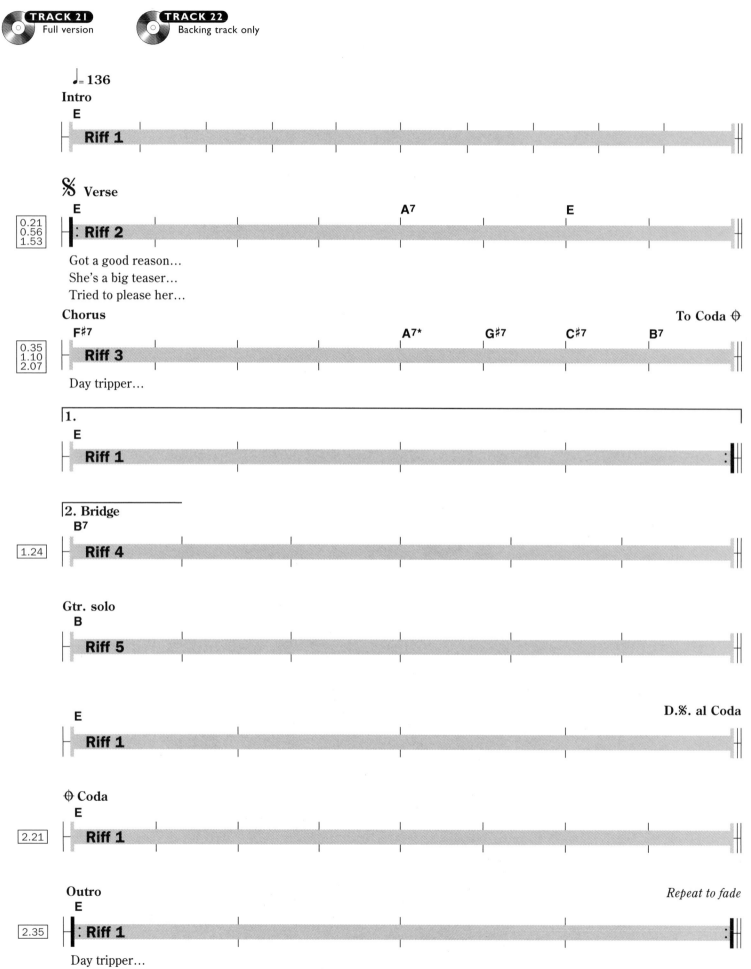

Riff by Riff...The Beatles *Page 20*

DAY TRIPPER
Lyrics

E A7 F#7 A7* `fr5` G#7 `fr4` C#7 `fr9` B7 `fr7`

Intro:	10 bars

E
Verse 1: Got a good reason
For taking the easy way out.
A7
Got a good reason
E
For taking the easy way out.

           F#7
Chorus: She was a day tripper
One way ticket, yeah.
       A7* G#7   **C#7**
It took me so long to find out
          B7
And I found out.

Instr: 4 bars

E
Verse 2: She's a big teaser
She took me half the way there.
A7
She's a big teaser
E
She took me half the way there.

           F#7
Chorus: She was a day tripper
One way ticket, yeah.
       A7* G#7   **C#7**
It took me so long to find out
          B7
And I found out.

Instr: 6 bars

B
Ah, ah, ah, ah, ah, ah.

Instr: 4 bars

E
Verse 3: Tried to please her
She only played one night stands.
A7
Tried to please her
E
She only played one night stands,
    now.
           F#7
Chorus: She was a day tripper
Sunday driver, yeah.
       A7* G#7   **C#7**
It took me so long to find out
          B7
And I found out.

Instr: 8 bars

E
Fade: Day tripper, day tripper, yeah.

DRIVE MY CAR

Words and Music by John Lennon & Paul McCartney
© Copyright 1965 Northern Songs.
All Rights Reserved. International Copyright Secured.

From the 1965 LP *Rubber Soul*, 'Drive My Car' has a strong R 'n' B feel and features bluesy harmonies throughout.

Every instrument plays a vital role in the arrangement of this song – there's no waffle, especially in the guitar parts which are, for the most part, single note lines. Once again we find the bass and guitar shadowing each other closely, with piano added on the choruses for extra depth. Once you've got past the opening syncopated riff the rest of the guitar parts should fall into place – be careful not to rush these guitar lines, they are (along with the bass) the foundation of the song.

Riff 1

This double-tracked, bluesy lick opens the track with a syncopated feel. The first notes you hear are not played on the downbeat but start on the upbeat. If you're having trouble counting this, just listen out for the drum fill to help bring you in. Use your third finger for the slide in bar 1 and play all the double-stops with a first finger barre on the G and B strings. Use a bright and slightly distorted sound.

Riff 2

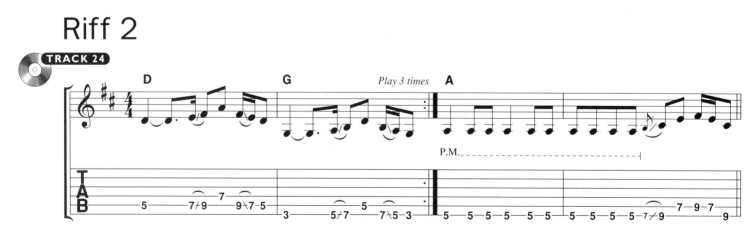

Riff 2 is an R 'n' B style single note line that is used in the verses. Use your third finger to play the slides and your first finger for the other notes.

Try to capture the rhythmic feel – it should be bouncy, with a slight swing.

Riff 3a

Riff 3b

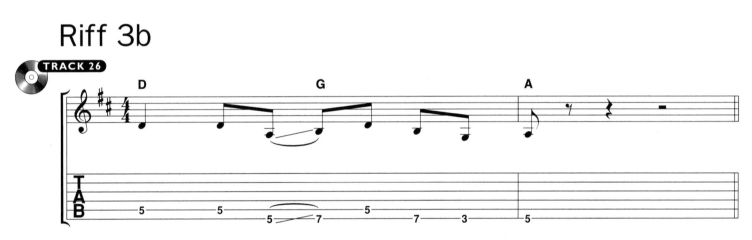

Riff 3a is another example of a simple chorus riff. This single note line follows the bass except for the phrase in bar 6 where there is more movement. Concentrate on the rhythm – you'll need to strike a balance between keeping the rhythm going and blending into the background. Riff 3b is used to link into the outro.

Riff 4

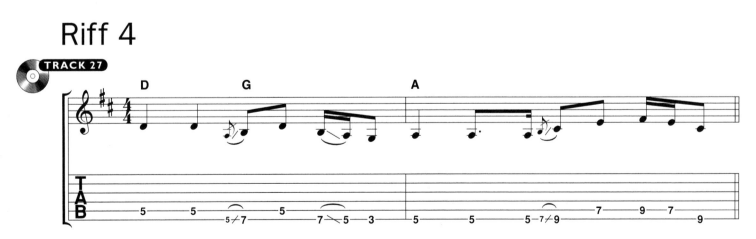

This outro riff is similar to Riff 2 so use the same fingering and rhythmic feel. If you are finding the position shifts difficult try shortening the last note of each phrase to give you more time.

DRIVE MY CAR
Riff Route Map

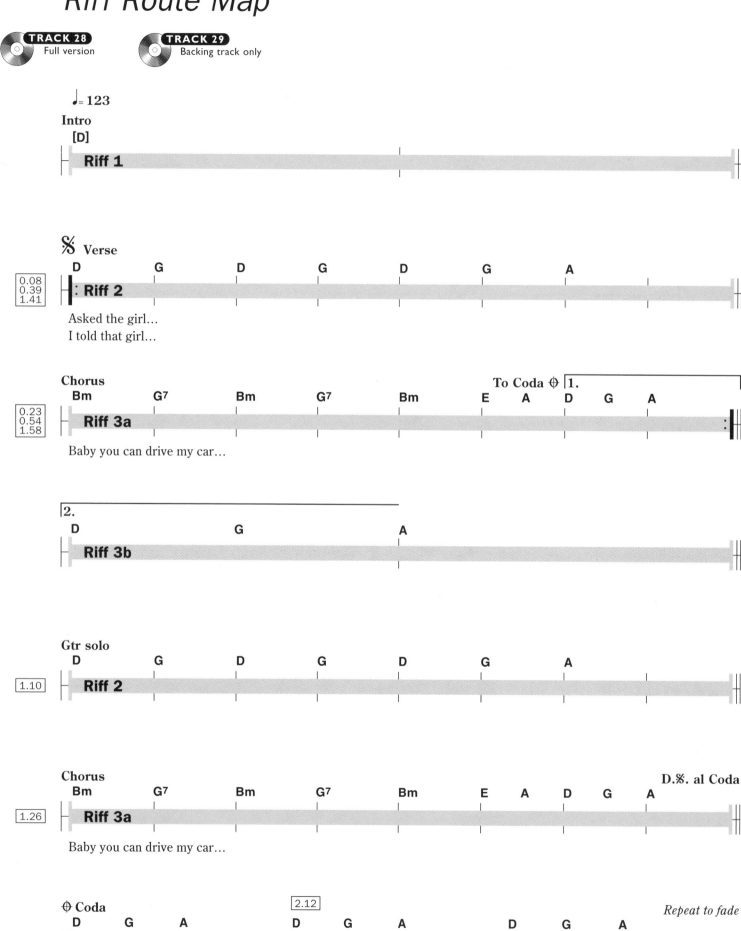

I FEEL FINE
Riff Route Map

TRACK 6 — Full version
TRACK 7 — Backing track only

♩= 180

Intro

D   C   G

Riff 1

𝄋 Verse

G   D

0.13 / 0.26 / 1.22   **: Riff 2**

Baby's good to me…
Baby said she's mine…

Chorus

C   G

0.21 / 0.34 / 1.30   **Riff 3** :

I'm in love with her…

Bridge

G^5 G B^5 Bm C^5 C*   D* G^5 G B^5 Bm   Am   D*

0.40 / 1.36   **Rhythm Riff 1**

I'm so glad…

Verse

G   D

0.50 / 1.46   **Riff 2**

baby buys her things…

Chorus   **To Coda ⊕**

C   G

0.58 / 1.54   **Riff 3**

She's in love with me…

Gtr. solo

G   D

1.04   **Riff 2**

                            D.𝄋. al Coda
                            (no repeat)

C   G

Riff 1

⊕ Coda   *Repeat to fade*

C   G   G

1.59   **Riff 3**   **: Riff 4** :

TICKET TO RIDE
Riff Route Map

TRACK 14 Full version   **TRACK 15** Backing track only

♩ = 124

Intro

| A | Asus² | A | Asus² | A | Asus² | A | Asus² |

Riff 1a

I

Verse

0.18

| A | Asus² | A | Asus² | A | Asus² | A | Asus² | A | Asus² | A | Asus² | Bm | E | E7 |

Riff 2

think I'm gonna be sad…

Chorus

0.27

| F♯m | D7 | F♯m | Gmaj7 | F♯m | E | A | Asus² | A | Asus² |

Rhythm Riff 1   Riff 1a

She's got a ticket to ride…

She

𝄋 Verse

0.42
1.31
2.19

| A | Asus² | A | Asus² | A | Asus² | A | Asus² | A | Asus² | A | Asus² | Bm | E | E7 |

Riff 2

1.3. said that…
2. think I'm gonna be sad…

Chorus

0.58
1.46
2.34

To Coda ⊕

| F♯m | D7 | F♯m | Gmaj7 | F♯m | E | A | Asus² | A | Asus² |

Rhythm Riff 1   Riff 1a

She's got a ticket to ride…

I

Bridge

1.13
2.02

2° D.𝄋. al Coda

| D5 D7 | D5 D7 | D5 D7 | E E7 | D5 D7 | D5 D7 | D5 D7 | E E5 |

Rhythm Riff 2

don't know why she's…

She

⊕ Coda

2.50

Repeat to fade

| A | Asus² | A | A | Asus² | A | Asus² | A | D7 | A | Asus² |

Riff 1b   Rhythm Riff 3

My baby don't care…

DAY TRIPPER
Riff Route Map

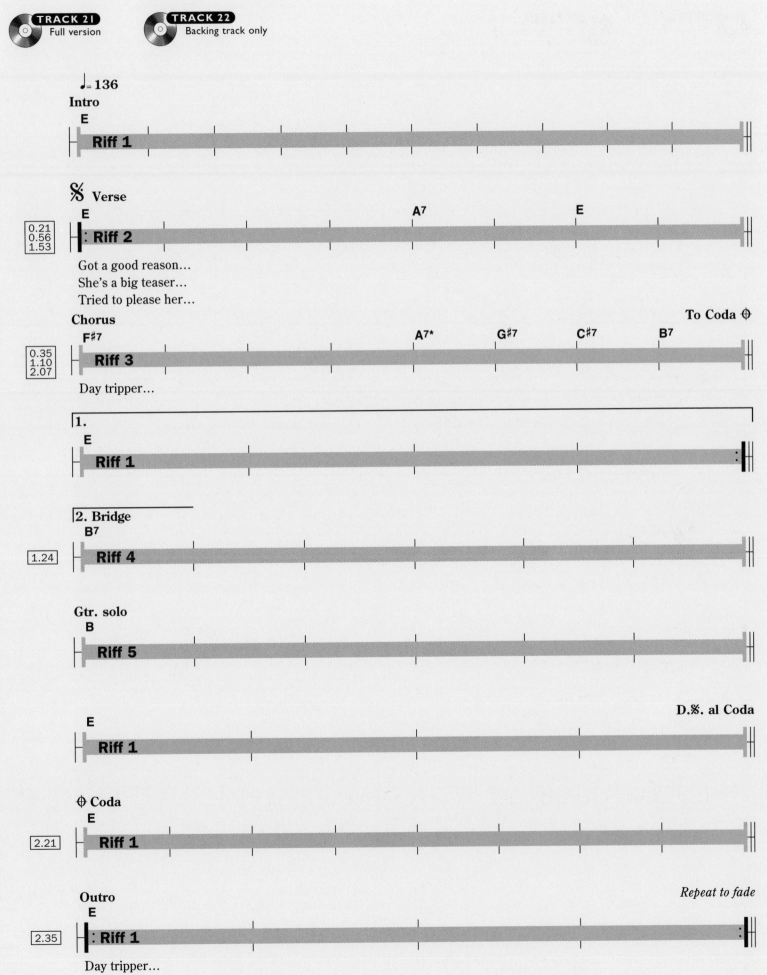

DRIVE MY CAR
Riff Route Map

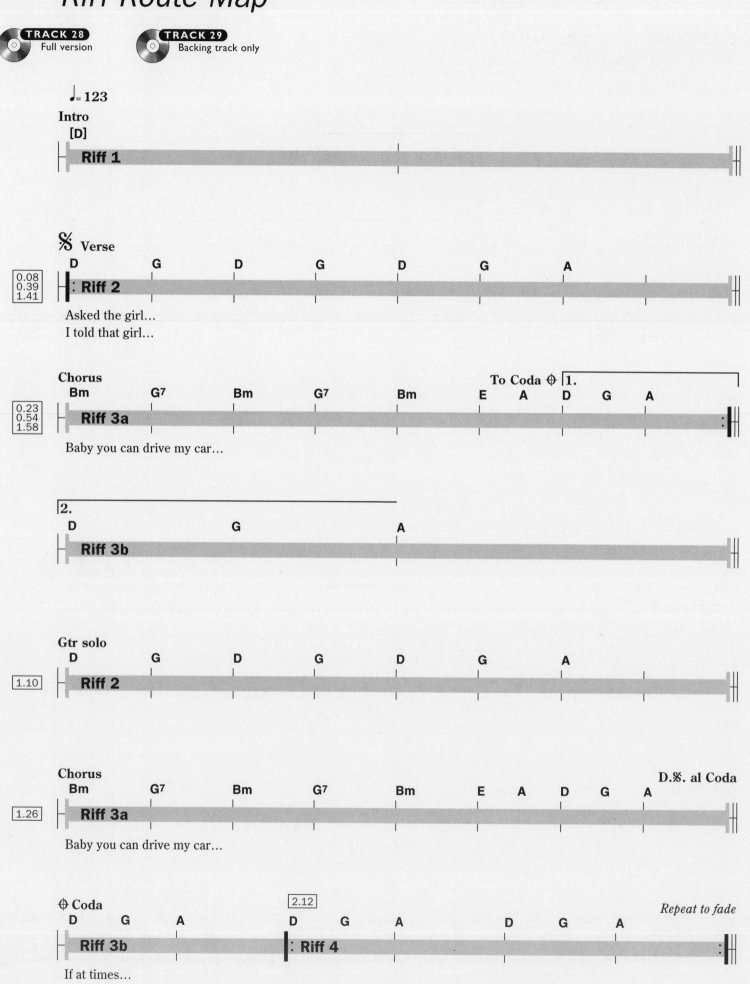

PAPERBACK WRITER
Riff Route Map

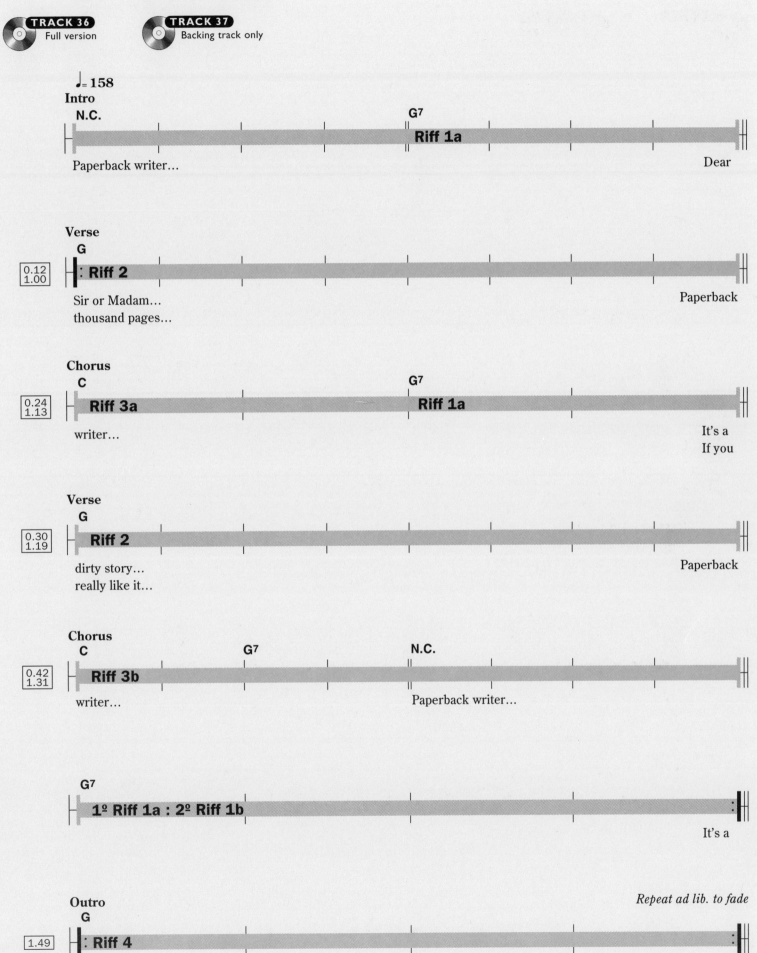

GET BACK
Riff Route Map

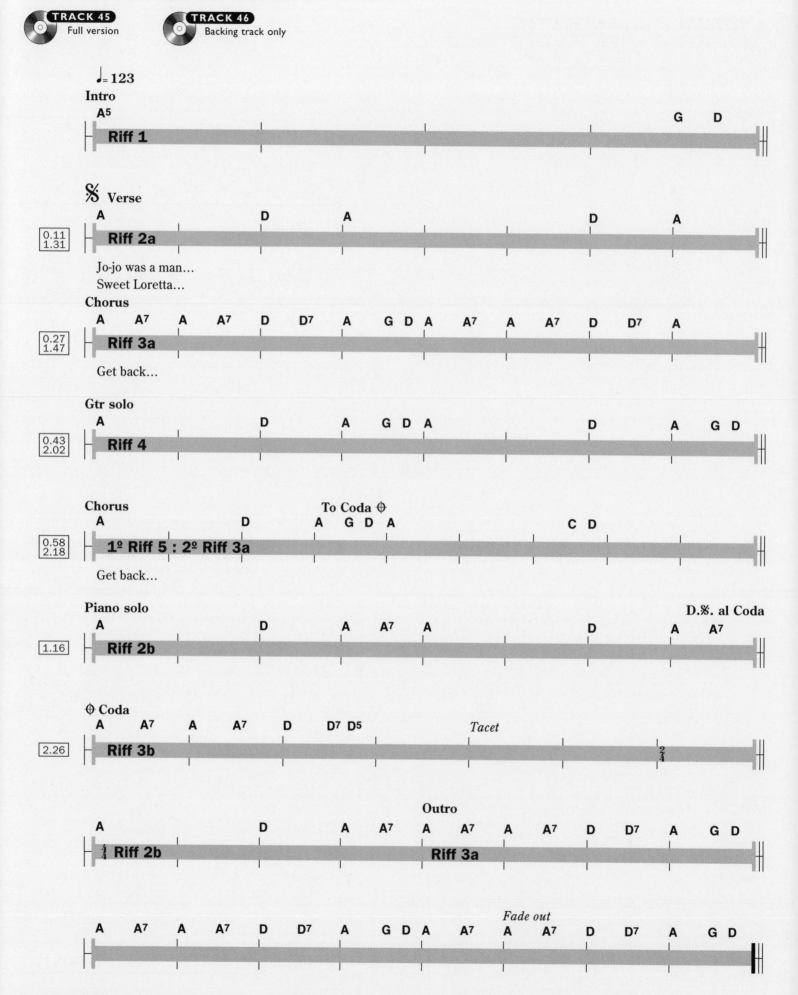

REVOLUTION
Riff Route Map

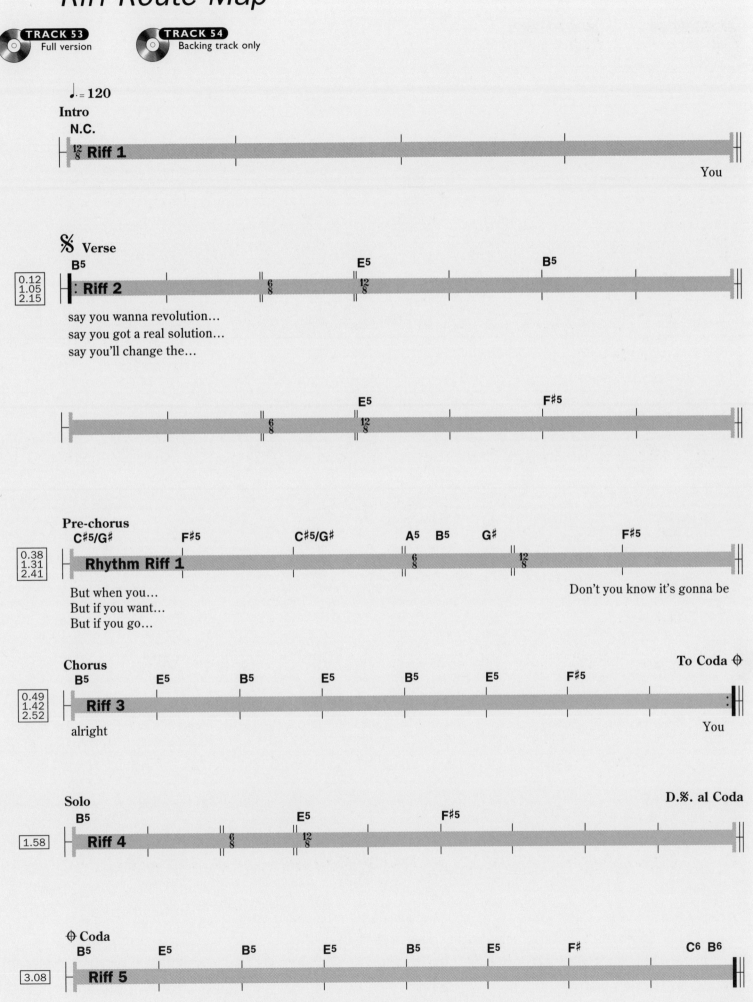

DON'T LET ME DOWN
Riff Route Map

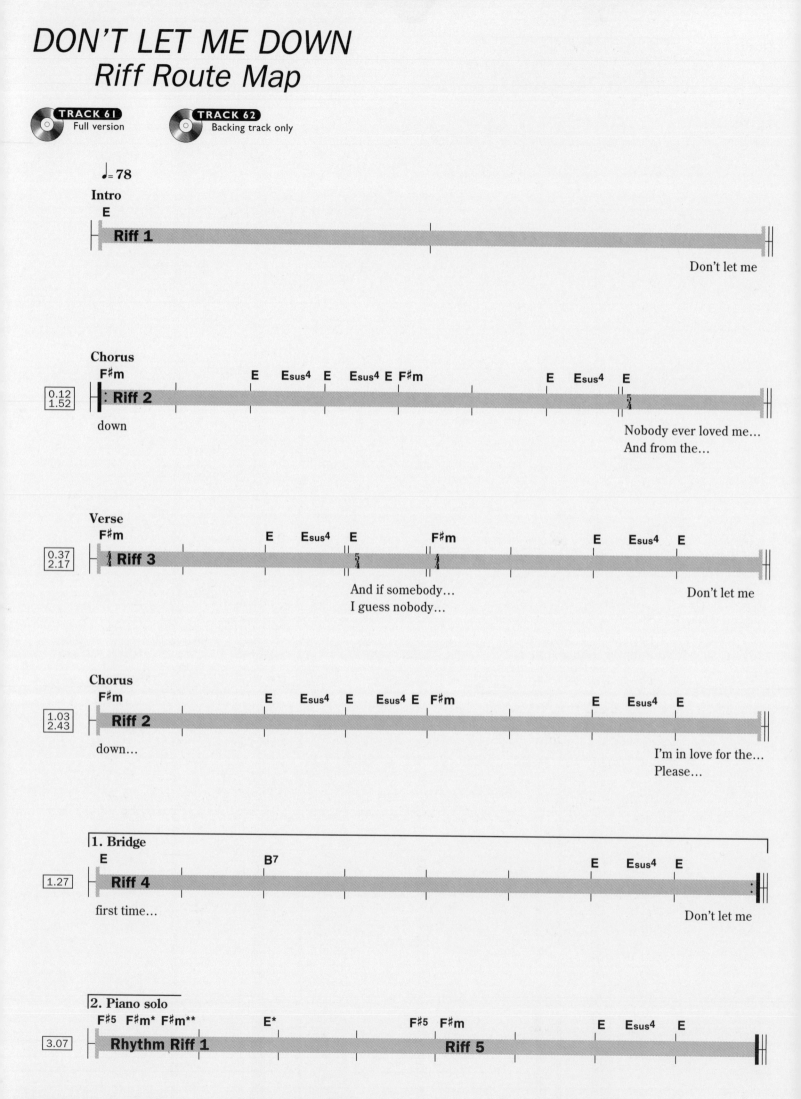

DRIVE MY CAR
Lyrics

D	G	A	Bm	G7	E

Intro: 2 bars

Verse 1:

    D   G
Asked the girl what she wanted to be
    D   G
She said "Baby, can't you see
    D   G
I wanna be famous, a star of the
         screen"
    A
But you can do something in
         between.

Chorus:

    Bm   G7
Baby you can drive my car
    Bm   G7
Yes, I'm going to be a star
    Bm   E
Baby you can drive my car
    A   D   G A
And maybe I'll love you.

Verse 2:

    D   G
I told that girl that my prospects
       were good
    D   G
And she said "Baby, it's understood
    D   G
Working for peanuts is all very fine
        A
But I can show you a better time".

Chorus:

    Bm   G7
Baby you can drive my car
    Bm   G7
Yes, I'm going to be a star
    Bm   E
Baby you can drive my car
    A   D   G A
And maybe I'll love you.

Beep, beep 'n' beep beep yeah.

Instr: 8 bars

Chorus:

    Bm   G7
Baby you can drive my car
    Bm   G7
Yes, I'm going to be a star
    Bm   E
Baby you can drive my car
    A   D   G A
And maybe I'll love you.

Verse 3:

    D   G
I told that girl I could start right
       away
    D
When she said "Listen babe, I got
      G
       something to say
    D   G
I got no car and it's breaking my
       heart
       A
But I've found a driver and that's a
       start"

Chorus:

    Bm   G7
Baby you can drive my car
    Bm   G7
Yes, I'm going to be a star
    Bm   E
Baby you can drive my car
    A   D   G A
And maybe I'll love you.

Fade: Beep, beep 'n' beep, beep yeah.

PAPERBACK WRITER

Words and Music by John Lennon & Paul McCartney
© Copyright 1966 Northern Songs.
All Rights Reserved. International Copyright Secured.

With its rich vocal arrangement 'Paperback Writer' displayed the singing skills of the Fab Four. The vocal harmony passages were certainly influenced by The Beach Boys, who were at the height of their popularity when this track was released.

While the vocals take this song to a different level, the guitar part is relatively simple and follows a style commonly used in earlier Beatles compositions. Each verse is introduced by a cracking guitar riff which then settles into a vamping accompaniment for the verse itself.

Riff 1a

This is a great riff and very easy to play if you use the correct fingering. You should use your first finger to barre the bottom three strings – this allows you to keep them ringing, then use the third and fourth fingers to play the other strings.

The sound should be twangy and distorted, (on the original it was probably a Rickenbacker) so use the bridge pickup with a bright, distorted tone.

Riff 2

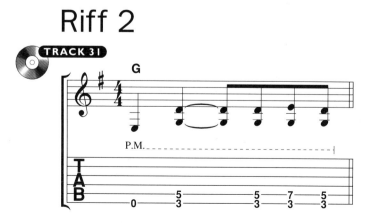

The guitar part for the verse is less obtrusive than for the intro. This is the kind of twelve bar riff that is very common in blues and rock 'n' roll. Play the basic chord with your first and third fingers and use the fourth to play the E note, muting the strings with your right hand.

Riff 3a

Riff 3b

These riffs are used for the chorus of the song (Riff 3b is an extended version of 3a). The last two bars of Riff 3b are similar to Riff 1, so use the same fingering.

Riff 1b

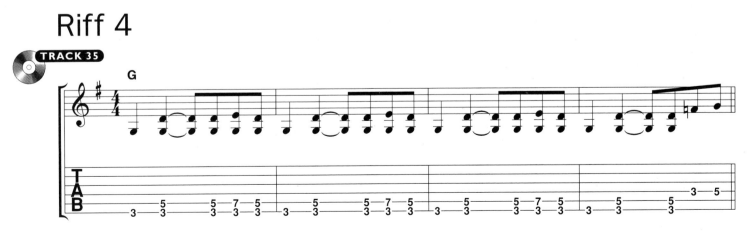

Riff 1b is a slightly altered form of Riff 1a, differing only on the last beat of bar 2.

Riff 4

This riff is basically the same as Riff 2, but as it's used for the outro section it can be varied a lot, using this basic pattern. The same fingering applies but this time don't mute with the right hand.

PAPERBACK WRITER
Riff Route Map

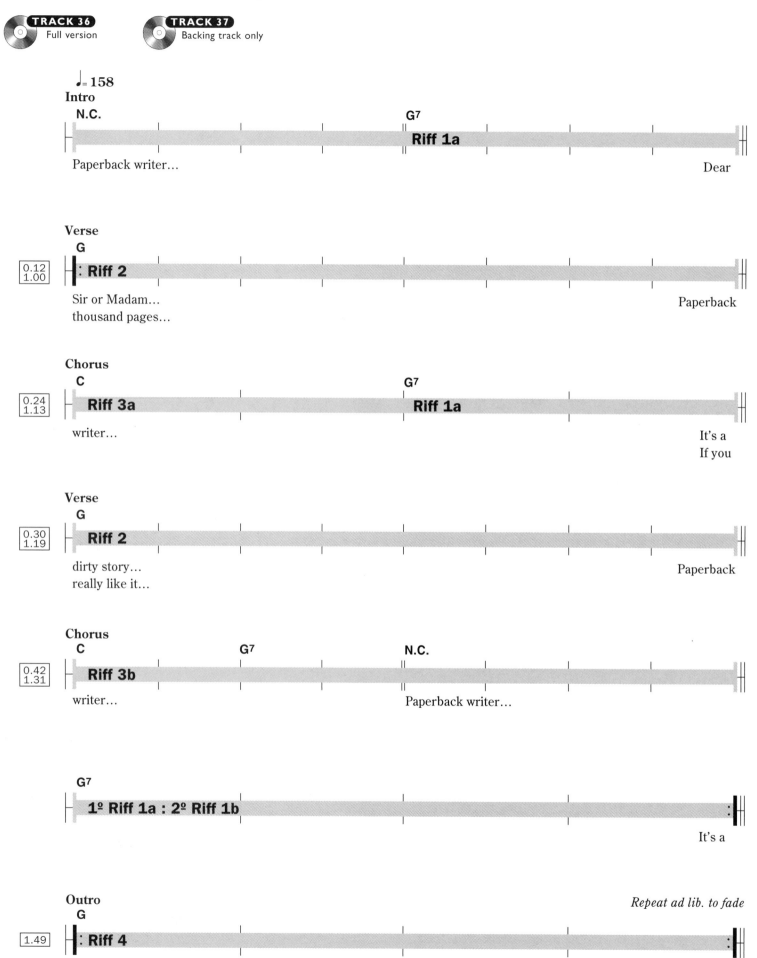

PAPERBACK WRITER
Lyrics

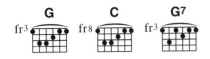

G   C   G7

fr3   fr8   fr3

Intro:
N.C.
Paperback writer

Verse 1:
G
Dear Sir or Madam
Will you read my book
It took me years to write
Will you take a look.
It's based on a novel
By a man named Lear
And I need a job

C
So I want to be a paperback writer

Chorus:
G7
Paperback writer.

Verse 2:
G
It's a dirty story
Of a dirty man
And his clinging wife
Doesn't understand.
His son is working for the Daily Mail
It's a steady job

C
But he wants to be a paperback
   writer

Chorus:
G7
Paperback writer.
N.C.
Paperback writer.

Instr:
4 bars

Verse 3:
G
It's a thousand pages
Give or take a few
I'll be writing more in a week or two.
I could make it longer
If you like the style
I can change it round

C
And I want to be a paperback writer

Chorus:
G7
Paperback writer.

Verse 4:
G
If you really like it
You can have the rights
It could make a million
For you overnight.
If you must return it
You can send it here
But I need a break

C
And I want to be a paperback writer
G7
Paperback writer.

Fade:
N.C.
Paperback writer.

"When I was a Beatle, I thought we were the best group in the goddamned world. And believing that is what made us what we were."
John Lennon

GET BACK

Words and Music by John Lennon & Paul McCartney
© Copyright 1969 Northern Songs.
All Rights Reserved. International Copyright Secured.

'Get Back' was released as a single in1969, and was
memorably featured in The Beatles' last ever live
performance, on the roof of the Apple building on
30th January 1969.

This song contains large elements of both Rock 'n'
Roll and R 'n' B but is played with such delicacy and
lightness of touch, it really becomes something else.
Once again, all the separate elements of the
arrangement are crucial, but none is overstated.
Once you've mastered all the riffs in this song
concentrate on emulating the laid-back feel of the
original; smooth position changes are vital in
sustaining the lazy groove.

Riff 1

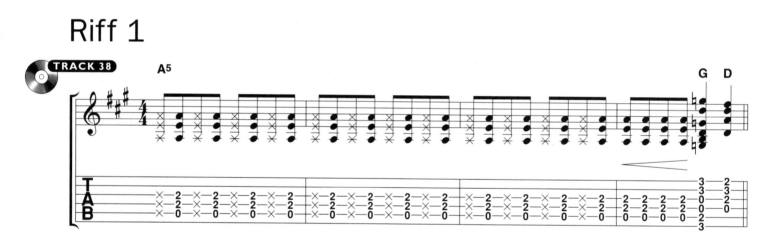

Riff 1 introduces the song with a repeated chord of
A5. Keep the shape of the chord as you play the
muted notes, lifting your left hand slightly to deaden
the strings. You should build gradually through the
riff, especially through the last bar to the G and D
chords. The sound is bright and slightly distorted,
using the middle pickup position.

Riff 2a

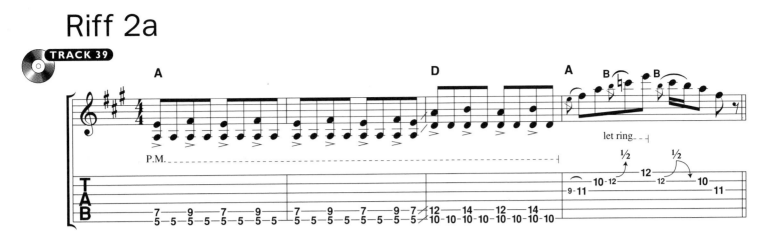

This riff is similar to the verse riff of 'Paperback Writer' and should be played palm muted with the fourth finger playing the F or B notes for each chord. Make sure that you accent the chords that fall on the downbeats. For the last bar use your third finger to hold the bend on the B string while you play the E on the top string with your fourth finger.

Riff 3a

This chorus riff combines a single note line and a high A7 or D7 chord shape. Notice how the single note line is played in the same position for both chords. The fingering works out neatly for this one; the A at the end of the single note riff should be played with the first finger, which leaves the others free to play the chords.

Riff 4

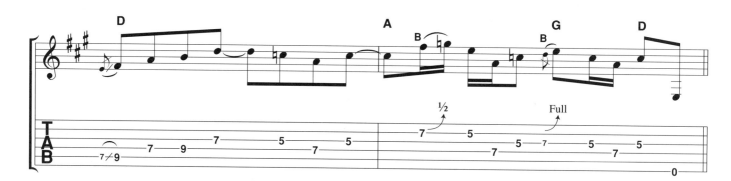

Riff 4 is a melodic solo which fits neatly over the verse chord sequence. In bar 3 there's a position shift in the middle of a phrase – use your first finger to play the D at the end of the first phrase, then, using the same finger, silently shift down to the fifth fret position to play the second phrase.

The string bend in bar 6 should be played with the third finger and supported with the first and second fingers, allowing you to hold it while playing the top notes as in Riff 2a.

On the repeat there's a similar solo with some variation so feel free to ad lib.

Riff 5

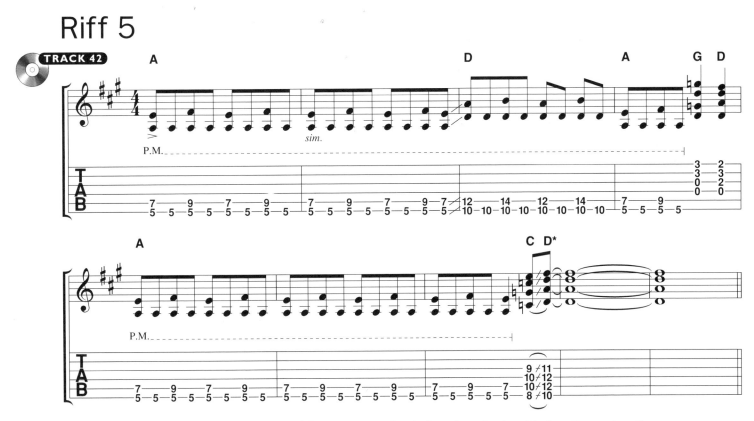

Riff 5 is used as an alternative part in one of the chorus sections. At the end of the riff, after the held chord, there is a short rest before the next section – listen out for the drum fill to bring you back in.

Riff 2b

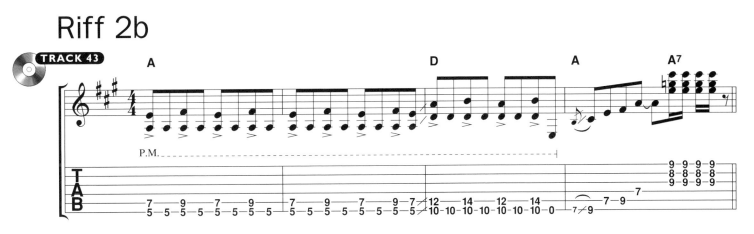

Riff 2b is used before the last chorus and combines elements of all the other riffs in the song.

Riff 3b

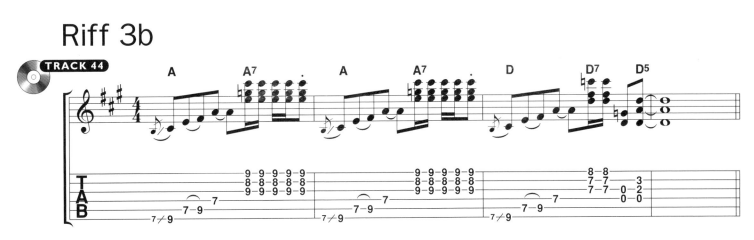

This is another version of the chorus riff, this time used to link the coda to the outro. Use the same fingering as for Riff 3a. If you follow the Riff map you'll see that there are three bars rest after this riff has finished. The third of these bars is in 2/4 and has a drum beat in it to help bring you into the next section.

GET BACK
Riff Route Map

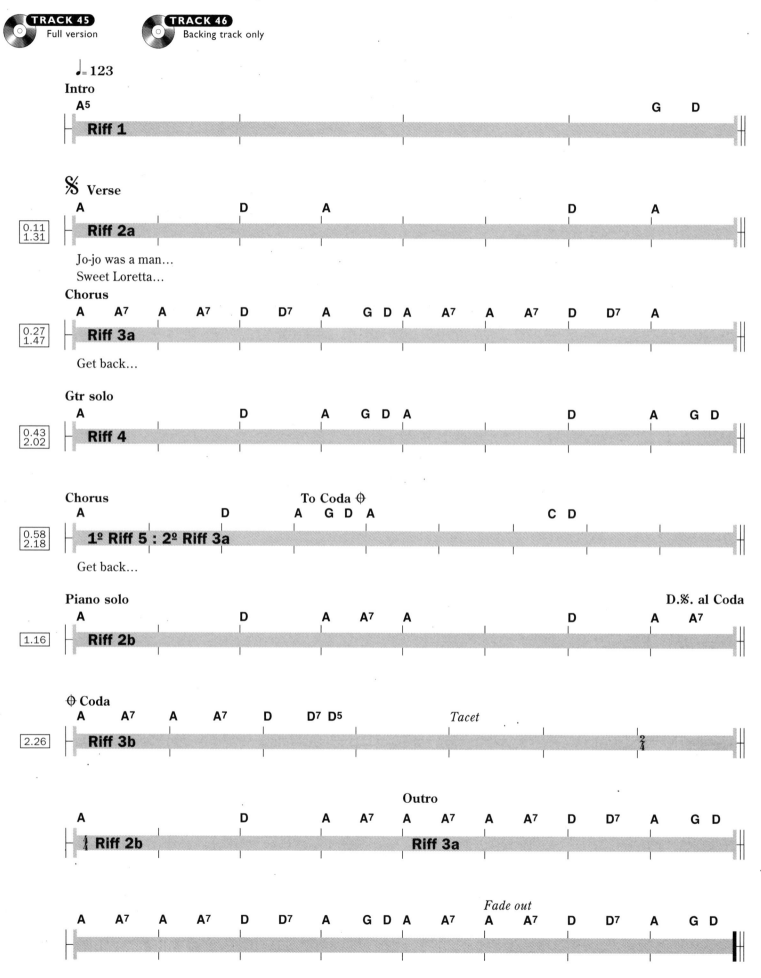

GET BACK
Lyrics

A   D   G   A7   D7   D5

Intro: 4 bars

Verse 1:
    A
Jo-jo was a man
Who thought he was a loner
D   **A**
But he knew it couldn't last
A
Jo-jo left his home in Tucson,
    Arizona
D   **A**
For some California grass.

Chorus:
    A **A7** **A** **A7**
Get back, get back
  D   **D7**
Get back to where you once
      A G D
belonged.
    A **A7** **A** **A7**
Get back, get back
  D   **D7**
Get back to where you once
      A
belonged.
Get back Jo-jo.

Instr: 8 bars

Chorus: Repeat

Instr: 8 bars

Verse 2:
    A
Sweet Loretta Martin
Thought she was a woman
D   **A**
But she was another man.
A
All the girls around her
Said she's got it comin'
D   **A**
But she gets it while she can.

Chorus:
    A **A7** **A** **A7**
Get back, get back
  D   **D7**
Get back to where you once
      A G D
belonged.
    A **A7** **A** **A7**
Get back, get back
  D   **D7**
Get back to where you once
      A
belonged.
Get back Loretta.

Instr: 8 bars

Chorus:
    A **A7** **A** **A7**
Get back, get back
  D   **D7**
Get back to where you once
      A G D
belonged.
    A **A7** **A** **A7**
Get back, get back
  D   **D7**
Get back to where you once
      D7 D5
belonged.
Get back Jo-jo.

A
Get back Loretta
D   **A** **A7**
Your mama's waitin' for you
        A   **A7**
Wearin' her high heeled shoes
A   **A7**
And a low neck sweater
D **D7**   **A G D**
Get back home Loretta.

Fade: *Repeat chorus*

REVOLUTION

Words and Music by John Lennon & Paul McCartney

The Beatles re-recorded this rockier version of the
White Album track for the B-side of the 'Hey Jude'
single, which went on to become the best-selling
Beatles 45 of all time.

Ironically, this comment on the late 60s is written in a
style from the previous decade, from the rollocking
opening guitar riff to the bluesy piano solo later on.
Despite these throwbacks the track has its
interesting twists and turns such as the odd 6/8 bars
and the dirty fuzz sound on the guitars! Don't be put
off by the 12/8 time signature, the song is still
counted in 4 but has a swung triplet feel to it.

Riff 1

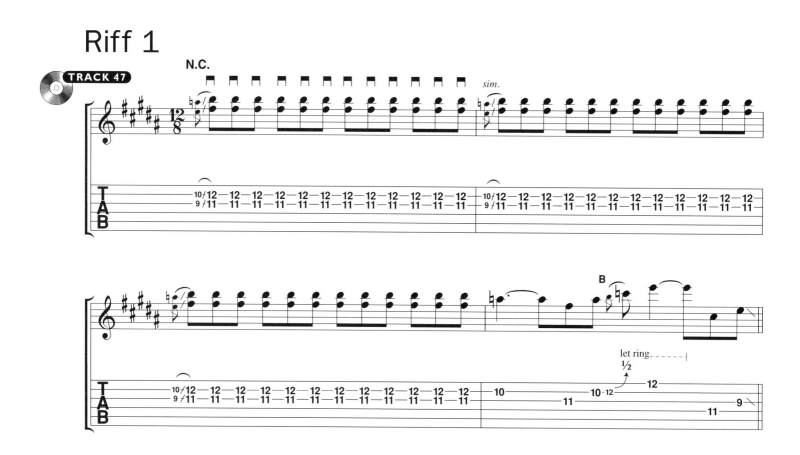

This is a real rock 'n' roll number and Riff 1, in
particular, shows a big Chuck Berry influence.
Although the sliding notes in the first three bars can
be played in several ways the easiest is to use your
second and third fingers – this will set up the hand
position you need for the last bar. In bar four use
your third finger to bend and hold the B string up a
half step while you play the top E string with the
fourth finger. The sound is full-on and fuzzy so use
the bridge pickup with plenty of distortion.

Riff 2

TRACK 48

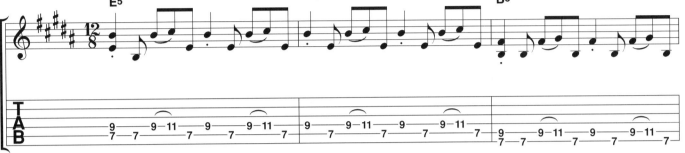

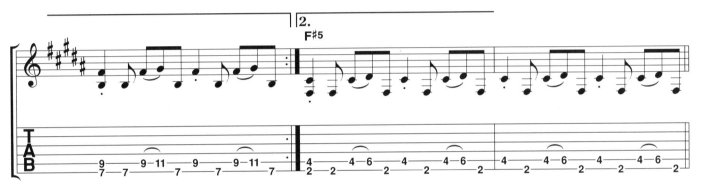

This 12-bar type riff is similar to the one used in 'Get Back', but a little more subtle. Instead of straight chords it is played as a single note riff with a loping, 12/8 rhythm giving the song a wonderful sense of movement.

Make sure you play the dotted notes short, as this is an important part of the feel of the riff. Watch out for bar 3 which is in 6/8 – if you think of the B chord as being played two and a half times you should be OK.

Rhythm Riff 1

TRACK 49

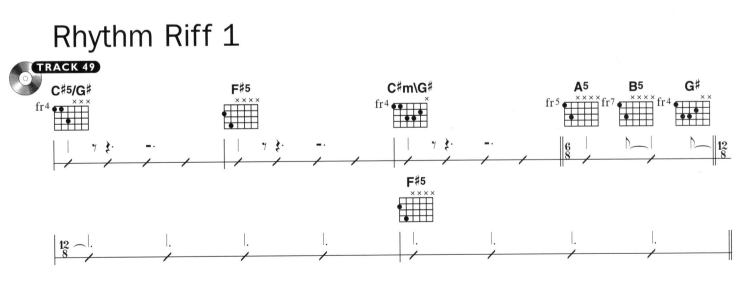

This simple chord riff is used in the pre-chorus. Again there is a 6/8 bar in the middle, but once you learn the movement of the chords you can forget counting and just play it by feel.

Riff 3

This riff is played high up on the fretboard, while another guitar holds down the rhythm, giving an extra lift to the chorus.

Use a first finger barre across the D and G strings and hammer-on with the third finger for the first bar; in the second bar slide and hammer-on with your third finger. The last two bars should also be played with a first finger barre, this time across the bottom three strings to enable you to keep them all ringing.

On the original recording there are two guitars in the right channel so you may find it difficult to tell them apart – on the accompanying CD these two parts are panned separately – you can hear this part clearly in the right channel.

Riff 4

TRACK 51

Riff 4 is very similar to Riff 2 in its content but has a
slightly different structure. Use the same fingering as
for Riff 2, and notice that the last four bars are the
same as the end of Riff 3.

Riff 5

TRACK 52

Play 3 times

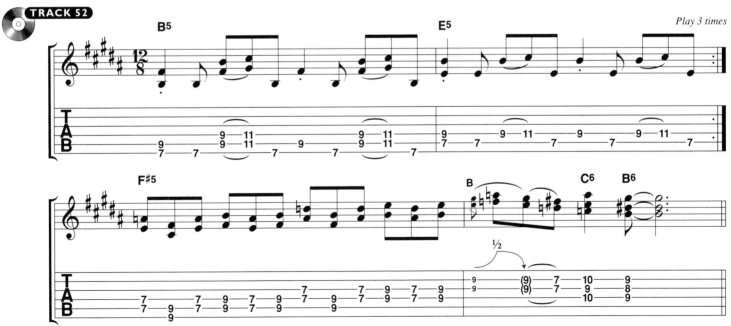

The double hammer-ons in bar 1 can be played with
your fourth finger by flattening it to hold down both
strings. The double stops in bar 3 should be played
by alternating a first finger barre with your third and

fourth fingers, while the double note bend in bar 4
can either be played with the third and fourth fingers,
or by flattening the third finger to barre the G and B
strings.

REVOLUTION
Riff Route Map

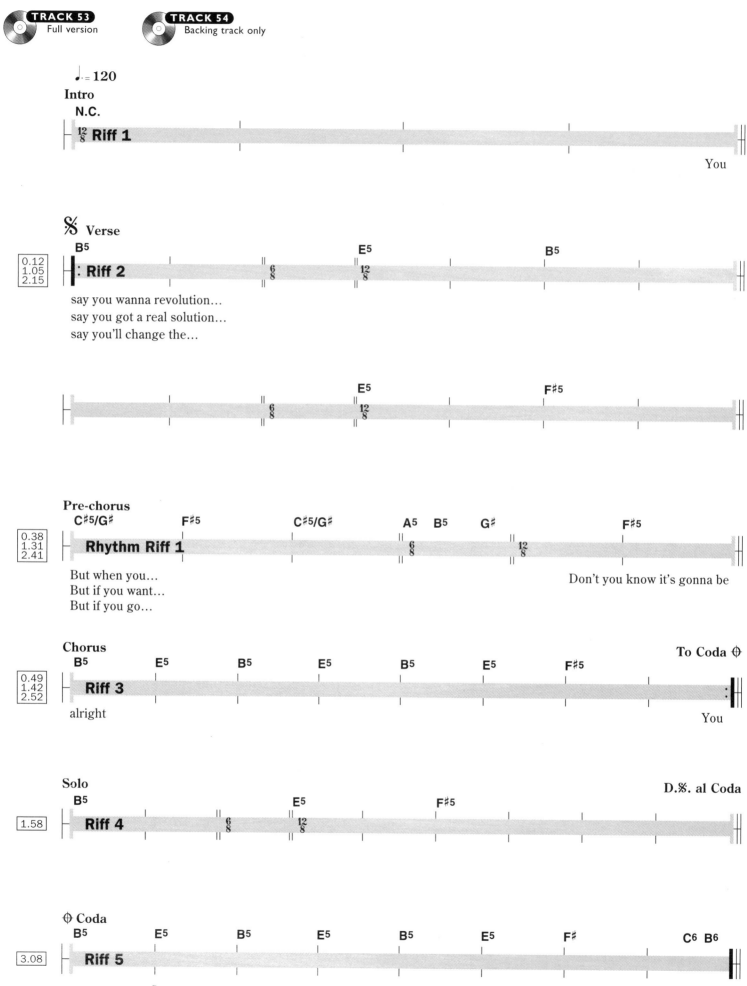

REVOLUTION
Lyrics

B5 **E5** **F♯5** **C♯5/G♯** **A5** **G♯** **C6** **B6**

fr7 fr7 fr4 fr5 fr4 fr9 fr8

Intro: 4 bars

Verse 1:
　　　　　　　B5
You say you want a revolution
　　　　　　　E5
Well you know

　　　　　　　　　B5
We all want to change the world.
You tell me that it's evolution
　　　　　　E5
Well you know
　　　　　　　　　F♯5
We all want to change the world.

Pre-chorus:
　　C♯5/G♯　　　　　　　　**F♯5**
But when you talk about destruction
　　C♯5/G♯　　　　　　　**A5**
Don't you know that you can count
　　B5　**G♯**
　　me out.

Chorus:
　　F♯5　　　　　　　　　**B5**
Don't you know it's gonna be
　　E5 B5　**E5**　**B5**　**E5**　**F♯5**
Alright, alright, alright.

Verse 2:
　　B5
You say you got a real solution
　　E5
Well you know
　　　　　　　B5
We'd all love to see the plan.
You ask me for a contribution
　　E5
Well you know
　　　　　　　F♯5
We're all doing what we can.

Pre-chorus:
　　C♯5/G♯
But if you want money for people
　　　F♯5
　　with minds that hate
　　C♯5/G♯
All I can tell you brother is you
　　A5　**B5 G♯**
　　have to wait.

Chorus:
F♯5　　　　　　　　　**B5**
Don't you know it's gonna be
　E5 B5　**E5**　**B5**　**E5**　**F♯5**
Alright, alright, alright.

Instr: 9 bars

Verse 3:
　　B5
You say you'll change the
　　constitution
　　E5
Well you know
　　　　　　　　　B5
We all want to change your head.
You tell me it's the institution
　　E5
Well you know
　　　　　　　　F♯5
You better free your mind instead.

Pre-chorus:
　　C♯5/G♯
But if you go carrying pictures of
　　F♯5
Chairman Mao
　　C♯5/G♯
You ain't gonna make it with
　　A5　**B5 G♯**
　　anyone anyhow.

Chorus:
F♯5　　　　　　　　　**B5**
Don't you know it's gonna be
　E5 B5　**E5**　**B5**　**E5**　**F♯5**
Alright, alright, alright.

　　B5　　　**E5**　　**B5**　　**E5**
Alright, alright, alright, alright
　　B5　　**E5**　　**F♯**　　　**C6 B6**
Alright, alright, alright, alright.

DON'T LET ME DOWN

Words and Music by John Lennon & Paul McCartney
© Copyright 1969 Northern Songs.
All Rights Reserved. International Copyright Secured.

'Don't Let Me Down' was the B-side of the 'Get Back' single of 1969. This track absolutely oozes quality with its rich, warm sound and laid-back groove.

Despite being based on only three chords, this song sustains interest with its odd 5/4 bars and lilting syncopations. Even straightforward bars of 4/4 are brightened up with different rhythmic patterns and accents. Take care not to rush the syncopated bridge section – the bass part plays virtually the same line so try to stick tightly to it.

Riff 1

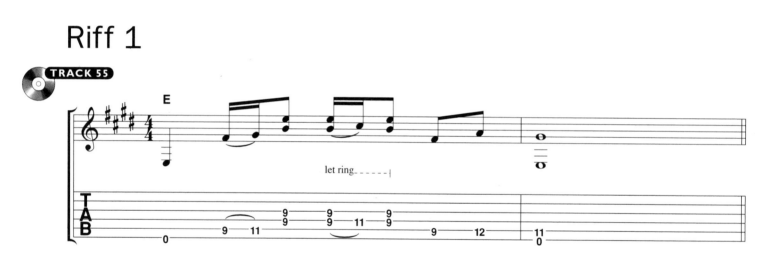

This short, country-style riff is used several times throughout the song. Use a first finger barre to play the B and E notes together – this frees up your third finger to play the hammer-ons. The sound is clean and warm so use the neck pick-up and aim for a laid-back and lazy feel.

Riff 2

In the first two bars keep the staccato chords short and choppy – this is a rhythm part, so leave plenty of room for the vocal. You can see Riff 1 appear in bars 3 and 4. In the second time bar, you'll have to hold the last chord through a 5/4 bar. Don't be thrown by this, just hold the chord and count to five!

"We reckoned we could make it because there were four of us. None of us would have made it alone, because Paul wasn't quite strong enough, I didn't have enough girl appeal, George was too quiet and Ringo was the drummer."

John Lennon

Riff 3

TRACK 57

This riff introduces some interesting rhythmic ideas – you'll find the first two bars easier if you count the quavers as 1 2 3, 1 2 3, 1 2. The stretch in the first bar is a little awkward – hold the A with your first finger and play the F♯ with the fourth finger which you then slide down to E while still holding the A.

It's high up the neck so it shouldn't be too hard. Hold the A again as you pull-off from the E to C♯, then use a first finger barre to play the A and C♯ notes at the fourteenth fret. The rest is straight forward except for another 5/4 bar. Once again, go for a lazy feel to compliment the vocal.

Riff 4

TRACK 58

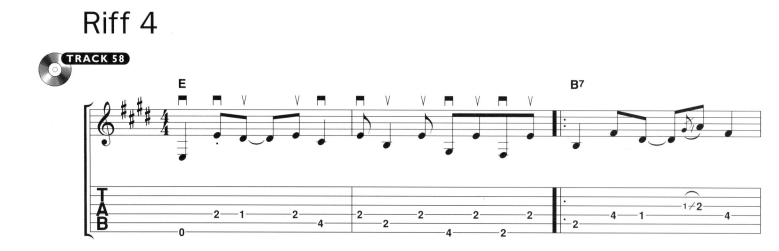

Riff 4 (cont.)

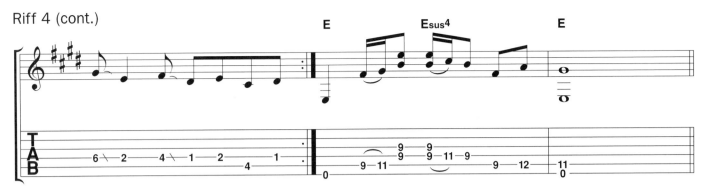

The bridge section, which is in this song is more like an alternative verse, has a single note riff which is played by both bass and guitar. If you look at the pick directions marked you'll see downstrokes for downbeats and upstrokes for upbeats – this will help you when you need to skip a string (as in bar 2). The portamento lines in bars 3 and 4 mean that you slide between the two notes, striking the lower note as you arrive. Once again Riff 1 makes an appearance to lead back into the chorus.

Rhythm Riff 1

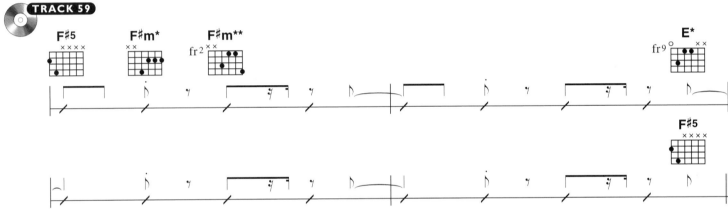

Used in the outro piano solo, the choppy chords of this riff are similar to Riff 2. The unusual E chord shape follows the pattern outlined in Riff 1.

Concentrate on the rhythmic feel – the guitar is playing a supporting role to the piano here, so try to merge into the background while still contributing to the rhythm.

Riff 5

Essentially this is an extension of Rhythm Riff 1 with another version of Riff 1 added to finish the song.

Keep the same feel going and use the same fingering for the last two bars as you did in Riff 1.

DON'T LET ME DOWN
Riff Route Map

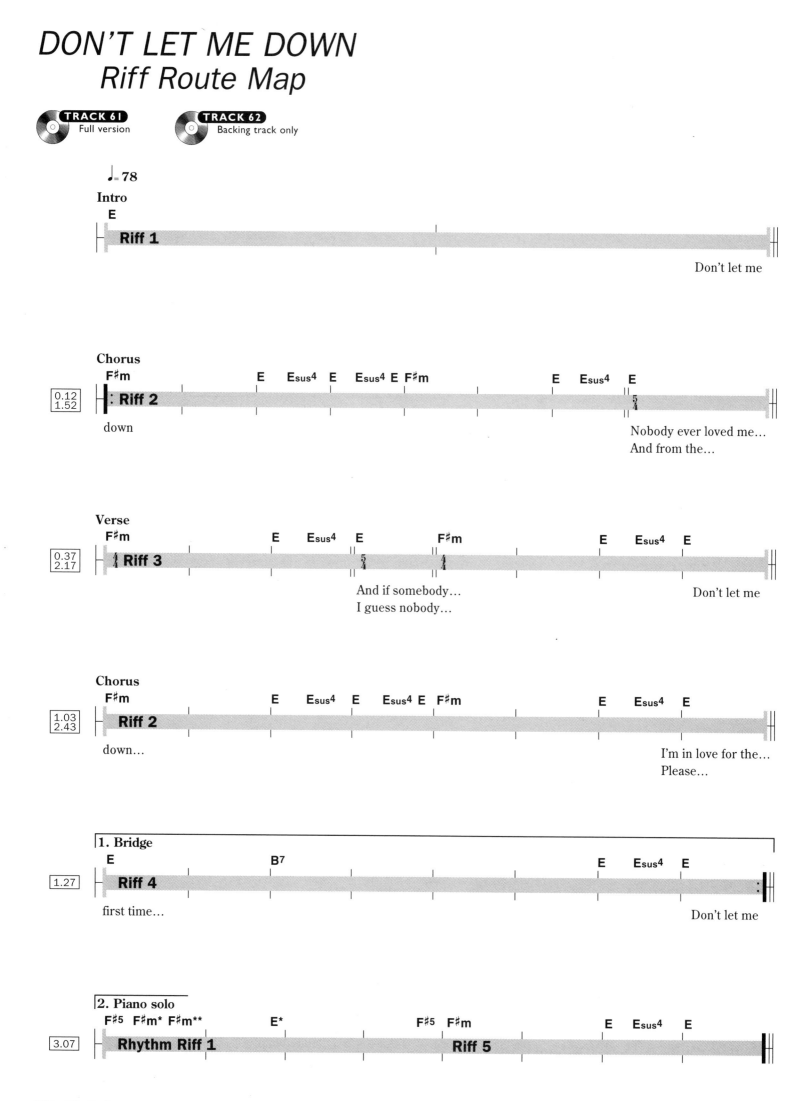

DON'T LET ME DOWN
Lyrics

E   F#m   Esus4   B7

Intro:

        E
2 bars

Chorus:

              F#m
Don't let me down
              E   **Esus4** **E**
Don't let me down
Esus4 **E**   **F#m**
Don't let me down
              E   **Esus4**
Don't let me down.

Verse 1:

      E   **F#m**
Nobody ever loved me like she does
                  E   **Esus4**
Ooh she does, yes she does.
      E
And if somebody loved me like she
        F#m
       do me
                 E   **Esus4 E**
Ooh she do me, yes she does.

Chorus:

              F#m
Don't let me down
              E   **Esus4** **E**
Don't let me down
Esus4 **E**   **F#m**
Don't let me down
              E   **Esus4**
Don't let me down.

Bridge:

      E
I'm in love for the first time
                    B7
Don't you know it's gonna last.
It's love that lasts forever
              E Esus4 E
It's a love that has no past.

Chorus:

              F#m
Don't let me down
              E   **Esus4** **E**
Don't let me down
Esus4 **E**   **F#m**
Don't let me down
              E   **Esus4**
Don't let me down.

Verse 3:

      E
And from the first time that she
        F#m
really done me
Ooh she done me, she done me
       E   **Esus4**
   good.
      E   **F#m**
I guess nobody ever really done me
Ooh she done me, she done me
       E   **Esus4**   **E**
   good.

Chorus:

              F#m
Don't let me down
              E   **Esus4** **E**
Don't let me down
Esus4 **E**   **F#m**
Don't let me down
              E   **Esus4** **E**
Don't let me down.

Fade: *Repeat chorus ad lib.*

GUITAR *signature licks*

The Signature Licks book/audio packs are especially formatted to give guitarists instruction on how to play a particular artist style by using the actual transcribed, "right from the record" licks! Designed for use by anyone from beginner right up to the experienced player who is looking to expand their insight. The books contain full performance notes and an overview of each artist or group's style with transcriptions in notes and tab. The audio features full-demo playing tips and techniques, as well as playing examples at a slower tempo.

ACOUSTIC GUITAR OF '60S AND '70S
by Wolf Marshall
00695024 Book/CD Pack $19.95

ACOUSTIC GUITAR OF '80S AND '90S
by Wolf Marshall
00695033 Book/CD Pack $19.95

AEROSMITH 1973-1979
by Wolf Marshall
00695106 Book/CD Pack $19.95

AEROSMITH 1979-1998
by Wolf Marshall
00695219 Book/CD Pack $19.95

BEATLES BASS
by Wolf Marshall
00695283 Book/CD Pack $17.95

THE BEATLES FAVORITES
by Wolf Marshall
00695096 Book/CD Pack $19.95

THE BEATLES HITS
by Wolf Marshall
00695049 Book/CD Pack $19.95

THE BEST OF BLACK SABBATH
by Troy Stetina
00695249 Book/CD Pack $19.95

BLUES GUITAR CLASSICS
by Wolf Marshall
00695177 Book/CD Pack $17.95

THE BEST OF ERIC CLAPTON
by Jeff Perrin
00695038 Book/CD Pack $19.95

ERIC CLAPTON – THE BLUESMAN
by Andy Aledort
00695040 Book/CD Pack $19.95

ERIC CLAPTON – FROM THE ALBUM UNPLUGGED
by Wolf Marshall
00695250 Book/CD Pack $19.95

THE BEST OF CREAM
by Wolf Marshall
00695251 Book/CD Pack $19.95

THE BEST OF DEF LEPPARD
by Jeff Perrin
00696516 Book/CD Pack $19.95

GREATEST GUITAR SOLOS OF ALL TIME
by Wolf Marshall
00695301 Book/CD Pack $17.95

GUITAR INSTRUMENTAL HITS
by Wolf Marshall
00695309 Book/CD Pack $16.95

GUITAR RIFFS OF THE '60S
by Wolf Marshall
00695218 Book/CD pack $16.95

GUITAR RIFFS OF THE '70S
by Wolf Marshall
00695158 Book/CD Pack $16.95

THE BEST OF GUNS N' ROSES
by Jeff Perrin
00695183 Book/CD Pack $19.95

JIMI HENDRIX
by Andy Aledort
00696560 Book/CD Pack $19.95

ERIC JOHNSON
by Wolf Marshall
00699317 Book/CD Pack $19.95

THE BEST OF KISS
by Jeff Perrin
00699413 Book/CD Pack $19.95

MARK KNOPFLER
by Wolf Marshall
00695178 Book/CD Pack $19.95

MEGADETH
by Jeff Perrin
00695041 Book/CD Pack $19.95

THE GUITARS OF ELVIS
by Wolf Marshall
00696507 Book/CD Pack $19.95

BEST OF QUEEN
by Wolf Marshall
00695097 Book/CD Pack $19.95

THE RED HOT CHILI PEPPERS
by Dale Turner
00695173 Book/CD Pack $19.95

THE ROLLING STONES
by Wolf Marshall
00695079 Book/CD Pack $19.95

BEST OF CARLOS SANTANA
by Wolf Marshall
00695010 Book/CD Pack $19.95

THE BEST OF JOE SATRIANI
by Dale Turner
00695216 Book/CD Pack $19.95

STEVE VAI
by Jeff Perrin
00673247 Book/CD Pack $22.95

STEVE VAI – ALIEN LOVE SECRETS: THE NAKED VAMPS
00695223 Book/CD Pack $19.95

STEVE VAI – FIRE GARDEN: THE NAKED VAMPS
00695166 Book/CD Pack $19.95

STEVIE RAY VAUGHAN
by Wolf Marshall
00699316 Book/CD Pack $19.95

THE GUITAR STYLE OF STEVIE RAY VAUGHAN
by Wolf Marshall
00695155 Book/CD Pack $19.95

0199